moon baboon canoe

other books by gary barwin

Franzlations: the Imaginary Kafka Parables (with Hugh Thomas and
 Craig Conley; New Star, 2011)
O: eleven songs for chorus (with music by Dennis Báthory-Kitsz;
 Westleaf Edition, 2011)
The Obvious Flap (with Gregory Betts; BookThug, 2011)
The Porcupinity of the Stars (Coach House Books, 2010)
frogments from the frag pool: haiku after Basho (with derek beaulieu;
 The Mercury Press, 2005)
Doctor Weep and Other Strange Teeth (The Mercury Press, 2004)
Killer Poodle Made Me Island King (Fox Meadow, 2004)
Raising Eyebrows (Coach House Books, 2001)
Seeing Stars (Stoddart Kids, 2001)
Grandpa's Snowman (Annick Press, 2000)
The Magic Mustache (Annick Press, 1999)
Big Red Baby (The Mercury Press, 1998)
Outside the Hat (Coach House Books, 1998)
The Racing Worm Brothers (Annick Press, 1998)
Cruelty to Fabulous Animals (Moonstone Press, 1995)
The Mud Game (with Stuart Ross; The Mercury Press, 1995)

moon baboon canoe

gary barwin

Mansfield Press

Copyright © Gary Barwin, 2014
All Rights Reserved
Printed in Canada

Library and Archives Canada Cataloguing in Publication

Barwin, Gary, author
    Moon baboon canoe / Gary Barwin.

Poems.
ISBN 978-1-77126-033-6 (pbk.)

    I. Title.

PS8553.A783M66 2014   C811'.54   C2014-900977-1

Editor for the Press: Stuart Ross
Typesetting & Cover Design: Stuart Ross
Author Photo: Gary Barwin

The publication of *Moon Baboon Canoe* has been generously supported by the Canada Council for the Arts and the Ontario Arts Council.

Mansfield Press Inc.
25 Mansfield Avenue, Toronto, Ontario, Canada M6J 2A9
Publisher: Denis De Klerck
www.mansfieldpress.net

your hearts will rejoice
and your bones will flower like young grass

—Isaiah 66:14 (trans. Marcia Falk)

... let the story of everything
End today, then let it begin again tomorrow.

—Mark Strand

contents

one
- Two Hummingbirds / 11
- Postcard / 12
- Time Machine / 15
- Civilization / 16
- A Squirrel Considers the Sky / 17
- Spring / 19
- Parade / 20
- Carrying Big Boy / 21
- Tragic Story / 22
- Song / 23
- Push and Pull / 24

two
- Woodland Road with Travellers / 27

three
- Top Floor / 37
- Inside / 38
- Hair Today / 39
- Moon Baboon Canoe / 42
- Belief Case / 43
- Bright Morning / 46
- Sonnet / 50
- Song / 51
- Planet Poetry / 52

four
- Seedpod Microfiche / 57

five
    Eclogging / 65
    Aubade / 67
    Handle a Platypus / 69
    Psalm / 70
    Protection Song / 72
    The Birds / 74
    Animal Intelligence / 76
    Song / 77
    Roof / 78
    Nature Poem / 79
    Coffee Shop / 80
    Toast / 82
    Hummingbird and Nonhummingbird / 83

one

one

two hummingbirds

we had never met:
two hummingbirds

on the inside of a star where
we were six-foot-three

each
casting our light

when we could not be sure
either of us

existed
like the two ends of a cow

to a cow though
we were almost endless

or like me and my great-grandson
born

a wing's-distance away
hummingbirds

on the luminous verge
of the beginning and end

postcard

the microscope sits on my desk
a gift from my father

a postcard from my mother
is placed under the lens

I'm 13
and love whales

the weather is beautiful
wish you were easier to see

*

I examine the postcard

the Brockdan Motel, 1973
Hwy 69, three miles
south of Sudbury

I look up close at the window
and you're in there

lying on the bedspread
gazing at ceiling tiles
their strange orange stains

*

1973 I dream
of prehistoric elves

sitting in circles
waiting for someone

to invent Elvish
then some wiseacre elf

opens his mouth
and speaks

but none of the elves
know what it means

*

you weren't really there
in the window

of the Brockdan Motel—
under the microscope

you are coloured dots
fields of inky texture

I'm a whale
inside me are elves

patiently waiting
rusting like leaves

I'll never love anything
as much as I love

this poem

time machine

after a line by Natalee Caple

dear friend
I have invented

a new kind of footwear
a third eye

also a time machine
I will save

the one you love
place hands

from the future
on his body

I open my eye
he opens his

each of us
seen from inside

civilization

for Carmel Purkis

We use our mouths to carry birds
We so often carry pitchforks

History is holes to fill
We so often carry birds

Our heads are marble busts in a museum
We hardly remember the missing limbs

We so often use the wind for a mouth
What is missing is also pitchforks

The mouth: birds made of pitchforks
a museum for farmers

Look through the mouth at the haystack of birds
filled with holes we think of as flying

We use our mouths to carry birds
We could carry pitchforks or kings

We spit birds out like the history of birds
Here: a ticket to the museum

a squirrel considers the sky

1

some say
stars are nuts

as if nuts
or stars

were words
in a wisecrack

but like squirrels
or stars

nuts are not always there
when you return

2

nuts
stars

a faint light
over the hill

once
there were many squirrels

3

wisecracks
then winter

nuts
then stars

outside squirrels
is everything

is no squirrel

our skin
deep sky

spring

Anne Frank now my grandmother's age
sings the hummingbirds

return to where the hummingbirds
belong in front of my house kids

between parked cars
my daughter reads

books always an empty coffin
open

parade

I understand what this sentence is trying to say
I empathize with each of its letters
its valiant full stop.
I believe in its I
I love its spaces
They are little animals
not yet extinct. Whispering
Between one thing and another
you and me
This sentence is my world

for now
Who am I
outside, looking in?
What was here before I?
What will be left when I is gone?

carrying big boy

Had to carry big boy
We were in the forest
He could go no further
What time was it?

Autumn
Hair tangled
Leaves
Deer-coloured

He could go no further
Bigger than me
The sun was lager
Slanting between trees

We walked through beams
Had to support him
"Hold my shoulders," I said

"Can't"
Had to lift him
Carried him
Could hardly walk

Soon night came
Black our mouths
Stars

tragic story

woman expects
tornado the father
baby the still eye

people worry
make quilts
picture cows and tragedy

then cow does fall
onto baby
from sky

but baby keeps growing
pink hand in muffled drum
swirl of leaves in forest

becomes an alp
stretches to clouds

so cow topples off
walks away
no mystery

song

old mother
do you know me?
I have not swum with you for years

I have been silent
these words I have learned
they are not words to trust

we were together when the moon rose
when my fists were soft as my tongue

old mother
here there are stars on the sky's wall

you did not expect me to live
I have said it
I will live

push and pull

the accordion flies aloft
it cannot rise

the accordion has nothing
neither locks nor teeth

it seizes the world
is imprisoned

it does not escape
does not live or die

the accordion finds no peace
its shadow bellows

without eyes, the accordion sees
tongueless, it speaks

the accordion loves another
hates itself

the accordion feeds sorrow
laughs at pain

the accordion
it burns and freezes

two

TWO

woodland road with travellers
(after brueghel)

for Kerry Schooley

1

they are small, walking away
the travellers with their burdens
men, women, some very old

they walk a road that was never a road
the travellers with their burdens
trudging through the shady wood

their children tramp beside them
or are carried in their arms
one girl with a moth instead of an eye

a woman with no legs but
a skirt of birds, and she moves like water
dark hair braided by tide

shit falls from a donkey
an old man carries a violin
they walk with only the leaves for song

distance invents itself with their moving

2

clouds and the rain from clouds
rain and the sound of rain
rain carried by the river and through
the stumpy hairs of grass

those who have become shadow
we call shadows

when it rains
there must be spaces
where the drops don't fall

3

in the distance
a bridge flows

you stand beside it
the stream goes nowhere
empty villages, taskless dogs

abandoned rivers without thirst or laundry
we try to hold the past inside us

but, as a man in a cart observes
at least one end of the donkey knows
it can't last

4

the woods both shadow and light
a road that isn't a road
words that don't say what they should

broken tree
a stump-like tongue
sky a donkey-coloured half-shadow
moth-light in the eyes

5

those in the kitchen whose minds travel
walking through forests
those who make toast and think of mountains
unwalking like forests

leaves that think of trees
the horizon which only exists from far away
time itself a leaf

in nature, the scientists say
beauty is created through death

we make things faster
we make things slower

you draw a line
knowing you'll have to cross it

6

this is what it is to live
a forest

I become geography
my hands go through

remembering
I walk into the yard

sit on the grass and look up

the sky has plenty
what: clouds? geography? memories?

7

my grandmother in her bed
her children, their children and
their children's children
gathered
her breath
her breathing

in the garden
leaves
leaving

we hold her breath
breathing

8

the traveller stands before
travel

wheeled vehicles and wayfarers
the final stretch of a woodland road
a luminous plain, a distant city

the traditional thoughts:
browns, greens, blue

a light-filled radiance
a rolling plain
a coach teeters on the ridgeline

moth eyes
a dip in the road
a steady course
low roads, turns, dead ends

detours
the trailing darkness
a recent storm
light-filled pools

three

top floor

stop eating my eye, Brother Worm
scarecrow, I invented the wind

dark like thought
I cut you in half

now two thoughts
stop eating my eyes, Brother Worm

a scarecrow body, a house of rags
worms eat the priests' eyes

antennae: I have none
my eyes inside Brother Worm

Brother Worm disappears
moves slowly to the escalator

but wind hogs the escalator
from the basement to the top floor
then down again

scarecrow, I invented the wind
Brother Worm does not ride

inside

inside Stephen Harper
there's a little dog

inside the dog
another dog

inside this dog
it's Stephen Harper

and inside him
a still smaller dog

in a Stephen Harper mask
(kidding, it's really Stephen Harper)

it's Stephen Harper
all the way down

Stephen Harper
why do you make things so small?

hair today

for Jeff Hawkins

1

I am a wild one

I razed the hairs of my wild face
mailed them

each to someone random
in the phone book

a beard is a river of mail
moving across the streets

feline as night
and the smoothfaced stars

2

the stars are holes in the receiver of night
listen:

the hairs of the quintessence
the godbeard of night
shaking out its owls, dark angels
its evening calls to loved ones
and death

3

an emergency

the dental work
the moon shapes
the lichen
the shopping carts
the Zohar of the beard

the armchairs
the stamp collection
the surround sound of the beard

the sacred text
the Fujiyama
the giant face of bees

the earth's trees
and mailboxes
its razor blade of stars and cochleae
its mail carriers
its undertow
is urgent

4

a crank call like a razor
whirring, breathing, scratching

"if you're so wild
why answer the phone?"

a black mist rising
a shadow through the shorn city
5 o'clock ellipses
7 o'clock commas
not words but
a thousand ant stigmata
crawling across the sky

5

each hair in an envelope falling
through the mail slot
a shadow inside a dove

beard only possible as
an agreement
between strangers

a rhizomatic face
cramming our brains with hair

6

we take our beard
a consensus of night
feed it into an ATM

we withdraw stars
wait for help

moon baboon canoe

a baboon rents a canoe
then smashes into the moon

fragments of moon, baboon, canoe
rain down

as you breathe your lungs fill with
moon, baboon, canoe

moon, baboon, canoe
inside each breath

people who I love, you say
people about whom I care

moon, baboon, canoe
moon, shoelace, canoe

baboon
baboon

belief case

1

the world is everything that is the briefcase

the hinge

shadow and ground
held together

papers inside
a tree

2

a briefcase
has two faces:

an inside that becomes
an outside

the origami of darkness
a handle on a cave
an origami of time as well as space

the face of the briefcase
the planet's laconic smile

3

a ring of briefcases
a henge

the eye casts no shadow
but is where shadows cast

4

a lung's worth of air
an archive of sighs

a lake without water
a lake's worth of water
looking for a bed

the cattle are lowing
the briefcase awaits

5

evolution expected the briefcase
but was surprised by water

wave
the briefcaseless hand
clap
the clasps of the hands

hands swim through
infinite wisps of paper

6

what is the difference between
a typewriter and a lion
a sheep and a briefcase?

driving past the fields:
—I see the sheep are shorn
—at least on the side we see
—ah yes. the outside

7

briefcases on the mountain
and the sky split by thunder

dark follows the hand
doesn't know what the moonlight says

night holds the earth by its black handle
walks

bright morning

1

there's something on the side of the road
I pull over to get a better look

it's small
a piece of dust

I take out my dictionary
dust:

a tiny part of something else
or several parts of something else

I'm on my knees
with a microscope

is it dusk or dust or a part of dusk
what once was a duck?

it glows with its own faint light
a single pixel

once part of something larger
I recognize you

this part of your face
pink but too small for smooth

I loved you in your mask
as you entered the store

2

the pixel is safe
in a shoebox

wrapped in tissue
kept warm

they say it was
part of something else

this pixel was once
on the wing of

a picture of something
on the other side of the world

carried by wind to become
your sad, hopeful

face
in a balaclava

3

o ballerina
my dolphin

everything in the dictionary
is just words

where does light come from
so small?

4

we said nothing
you gave me your gun

I watched your back
in the security camera

and the bells of the door
jangled

5

where was I going
when I found you?

to the duck pond with bread
to the library for books
to the forest with the dog?
I was driving

at first I cannot read
by your pixel light

then one morning
I stop trying

go outside
load you into the gun

o bright morning
o bright morning song

I pull the trigger
and you're gone

sonnet

Delete this line.
Delete this line.
Delete this line.
Delete this line.

Delete this line.
Delete this line.
Delete this line.
Delete this line.

Delete this line.
Delete this line.
Delete this line.
Delete this line.

Delete this line.
Delete this line.

song

outer space don't
believe in it paper clips

should be important something just
whizzed by

death imagine a kite
that's all string

all right enough imagining
if you haven't seen a lizard squirt

blood from its eye
you haven't lived

tiny owl on the windowsill
breath of invisible trees

ghosts don't believe in them
so my family gathers round

they sing to me
then it's the end

planet poetry

for M. D. Dunn

I rise then fall
remember when I was born

I wear the ocean like a dress
shores like skin

the Great Lakes like wolves
when I was an owl the twilight

the twig light of forest
now lightning

shoots from my head
into the sky

antlers of thunder
rise and fall

my mouth a storm
my tongue a cloud

I don't know what size things are
do I carry the ship

or does it carry me?
I wake to my life-green life

where the mall grows
the townhouse edges of town

who can believe your molecules
mountains

moleskins or
foldable chairs?

I leap and
for an instant

I am the citizen of no planet
a lungful of air

nuzzling stars
and then

four

seedpod microfiche

1

a grass blade, a truck
a small son
a constellation

evolution is an oblong song
the fishes whisper

seedpod, microfiche of twilight
a dewdrop observed, a cobweb
a weed-wrapped tongue or treetop

bulrush, an art song
consciousness
a fossil 8-track of the city

there is, my love,
a stethoscope whose end
is nowhere
whose earpieces
are everywhere

2

a glimmering blade, a small truck
a grass son, a constellation of lines

evolution is a long song
whispering fish

the sewn seed is dropped twilight
microfiche an observation tower for wings
weeds, a rupture of the tongue

bulrush consciousness
a molecular tower
the roseate backing track to the city

there is my love for a stethoscope
whose raptor
is everything

3

glass braid of the eclipse
winter makes smaller our small sun
for whom consolation
is everywhere
a song of longing
whispered between fiche and phone

seedpod is the nape
of springtime on the map of trees

[insert song here]
a fossil
an earnest stethoscope
but no end

4

the last bidding of the lips
a consternation of sun

a long song
paths of fish through the whispers
of elevators and seabeds

seed is the mitosis of sleep

dew on the rabbit
nap of the tongue
twilight braided through an owl

injured by song
or inured to it
strangers are fossils
stethoscopes with no eyes

5

the truck, only four, asks
what else would stars do but constellate?

the solution?
whisper-like fishes

paws of twilight microwave
cobwebs wrapped like weeds or a rush
around the young

an experienced guide can follow
8-tracks through the city
the way a scientist follows
an atom's breath

love like a stethoscope
with neither ears nor heartbeats

6

glass stuck in the foot
a small revolution

the immolation of whispers
a barbican of fish

matter grows from light
a cobweb its own misery
dusk on the owl of the tongue

a fossil records its own memory

a stethoscope whose end
is its beginning
and whose beginning
is also twilight

five

eclogging

Nature, I hate you
and your petty flummoxing of the butterfly's wingdust
your immersive credo is irritating
your pneumatic pontificating does nothing to assuage the oxidizing
    Chevy of the red-shifted subdwarf sternum-thumper that is
    upper management and my heart
the unrelenting entropic cadenza of your rococo filibustering
your cantankerous obfuscations—like winter, or autumn
are like the brain's catamaran
an oxymoron
or an oxytocin
the exact taxonomy unclear but proximate to the irradiated tocsins of
    the deoxyribonucleic aficionados of the Spirographic Lite-
    Brite drive-through of the 21st century
your tune-carrying maw is a vector for collusion
your vainglorious banquet of pockets, numinous, piping, populous
    and astringently verdant with acquisitive glimmer

Nature, you brindled Mixmaster
tastemaker
gene marker
your precipitate pox of clouds, no-see-um nano deer, ocean flux of
    quiddity and riboflavin
the catholic prestidigitations of your carbonara miracles
the peroxided phlox of your tuskless barnacles
make me your amanuensis only
a portico for your amusement and your fissured and warty biome-
    busy solipsistic landforms

I don't want your Bisquick sustenance
the parti-coloured borders between me and you
some ecotwittered mastication of self, salt water, and elementary
        particles
Your greasy baster injects my sorry canticles with lassoed protoplasm
I'm a borrower of furrows in the forests of your phylacteries

Nature, because of you, a profusion of fission-ready Midget Fighting
        League lions are ready to frack my Oronoco-infused hashtag-
        rich limb-jungle vein-doilies rendering the Antarctic
        taxidermy of my soul's subterranean knife block, a geodesic
        Isaac Brock triumph of isometric 1812 plate-tectonic
        platitudes

I hate you, Nature
you emasculate the tusk of my finger holes
and leave me parking

aubade

a car door slams
a rainy street

here we are a room
surrounded
here break our teeth on fire

here we discover a bear
snare a river
we balance the ocean on our tongues

here the waves slick our nipples
here we go to sleep in sagebrush
here we are outside

one eye doesn't know
what the other eye is doing

self-portrait carved from the inside
a grocery store built by paper bags and tender fruit

its tweezers, shoe polish, and cashiers
awake later than us

box spring in autumn
snow like a business letter

planets
plants
a river

rock
lullaby
pinnacle

the slug turns over
its back wet with sky

danger
the night
a lullaby

handle a platypus

a woman is giving birth
handle a platypus

a man jumps off a ridge
handle a platypus

the world is waiting
handle a platypus

handle a platypus
only in an emergency

sad rocket ship caged
by the ribs' leafy warning

psalm

I don't want to admit it
but I've been a bad sheep

for they let me lie down on the sweet lawn
helped me to speechless waters
restored my painful feet

they led me down garden paths that were not ironic
or filled with worrisome garden gnomes
but lit upon the shed of happiness

I've walked in death shade, in night valleys
in paddocks where invariably I was dark
yay! as my niece says sarcastically
and because they followed me I didn't fear evil

and wasn't overwhelmed by death
when my thoughts were my enemies
they made reservations in a nice restaurant
and the entire staff obligingly filled my wine trough

picked up my napkin and called me a nice salmon
so when I next catch sight of Marsha and Fred
the two hyperintelligent apes who have shadowed me
with their Etch A Sketch drawings all the days of my life

I shall shake, shake with colossal vigour
disquieting their continuous knob-twisting with my furious hooves
There shall be no never-ending ape-directed silver lining
for my hillock cleaving will be fearsome to both hoggets and apes

my fleece shall be as a wolf upon my howling spine
and I will dwell in the my-parents'-basement of my own self for ever
one woolly shoulder pushed against the mutinous wheel of these my
      mutton-fated days

protection song

after Al Jolson

O birth of many babies
clarinet playing
and the blackfaced river
how I love you

the trees are Jews
birth
leaves
in autumn under water

the sky in the river
in the river under water
beside clouds that flow in water
under the pine, beside the oak

a crowd of friends marvelling at ships
fear of death
a fear of death beside you
parents, wife, children, friends

those whom you wish had no death
that they sail on the river
on the sky sailing in the river
those that sail endlessly and without fear

O sky-faced baby
blackfaced Jew and Jewfaced black
who will protect you

the birds swimming
the banjos soft and low

the birds

after Todd Rose

no pair of birds
should ever
be seen
as being just
or necessary
and no result
of a pair of birds
should ever
be seen as
a victory
or success

every pair of birds
should be understood
as a tragic
failure
of catastrophic
proportions
a failure of birds
to act
with intelligence
creativity generosity
kindness faith
and respect

in the end
we will remember
not the birds
of our enemies
but the silence

animal intelligence

certain moths drink the tears of sleeping birds
birds sleep the dark fist of moth's wings

wings herd the wheeling eyes of deft mutes
mute desks sleek the cloud of sterns' wheels

wheels Hebrew the horse of hard times
whoever mouths the tides' breast is the forest

and my friend:
on the necks of sleeping magpies moths observed

the proboscis an ancient harpoon
inserted in feathers

they do not know the tear-drinkers
the nutrition of stars, the footsteps

song

the sun has found its little bed
the oxen have stopped plowing
O potato of my heart
the knife tomorrow

roof

room in
which in love with
I am
in my house as
the sun containing
barely itself across
its little box goes
illuminating
a couch on which
sleeping
the dog is
eye twitching in
walk roofers as
dream
the roof next door

nature poem

even on the sidewalk
I want to be a nature poet

this summer light is nature
so is the air and
the rain-soaked road

scooping up after my dog
the bag warm as my dog's insides
is nature

yes it's nature inside
and out
here in Hamilton, Ontario

nature inside and out
this poem

coffee shop

in the hotel of non-existence
the VACANCY sign flashes

I've a room there
and a broken TV channelling

only me
the famous show of no-shows

in the coffee shop
they don't serve coffee

I order
a cheese sandwich

the waitress
serves dinner

to another table
and I say

in a cheese sandwich
I am the absence of ham

without a cheese sandwich
there's no proof that

I am
and she says

you've been here since
before you were born

and what's worse
you've always been

a lousy tipper
I wait until closing

then walk to my room
through their greasy little windows

the stars sparkle
with butter and expectation

I sing to myself
or the other way round

toast

Toast pops out of Toaster
and Old Man Snake
passes him to Betty
now Betty is beautiful

Betty passes Toast to Bird
Bird turns blue
Bluebird we will call her
until we think of something better

Bluebird tries to pass Toast to Fred
but Fred doesn't notice because
he's reading the paper
—poet makes headlines again!—

finally Fred takes Toast
the hairs of his chin become smoke grey
we're not sure what to call him, 'old,' maybe
his beard a thicket of ashen life

then Fred sticks Toast
back into Toaster
pushes the lever and
Toast returns

hummingbird and nonhummingbird

for hummingbirds
the end

resembles dust
then more hummingbirds

dust between
hummingbird and nonhummingbird

for hummingbirds
the end

dust between
hummingbird and nonhummingbird

dust
then more hummingbirds

notes & acknowledgements

"Postcard" is from a postcard sent by Martha Baillie as part of a project associated with her novel in progress.

"Time Machine" is for Nikki Reimer in memoriam her brother Chris. It was first published in *The Week Shall Inherit the Verse*.

"Civilization" is after a sculpture by Bai Yiluo and appeared in *The Rusty Toque*.

"A Squirrel Considers…" was published in the chapbook *our hircine, murine doppelgängers, mars* (phafours press, 2013).

"Carrying Big Boy" is after the *Ecce Homo* repainting by Cecilia Giménez.

Thanks to Miekal And for sharing the Wisconsin news report behind "Tragic Story."

"Push and Pull" is after a poem by Thomas Wyatt.

"Woodland Road with Travellers" is in memoriam my friend, Hamilton writer Kerry Schooley (1949-2010). It previously appeared in *Grain*.

"Bright Morning" appeared in *Branch Magazine*.

"Seedpod Microfiche" appeared as a chapbook by above/ground press.

"Psalm" is based on Psalm 23 and appeared in *The Puritan*.

"Protection Song" is for my father and emerged from a writing activity by Gabriel Gudding.

"Animal Intelligence" is based on the article "Moths drink the tears of sleeping birds," by Debora MacKenzie, *The New Scientist* (December 20, 2006).

"Coffee Shop" is after Mark Strand.

"The Birds" and "Song" previously appeared as lyrics to songs by Dennis Báthory-Kitsz in *O: Eleven Songs for Chorus SATB* (The Westleaf Edition).

thanks

to the editors and readers of the publications where some of these poems first appeared

to the reading series and their audiences where many were performed

to the supporters of public funding for the arts for help in the writing, publishing, presentation, and promotion of these works as well as the vibrant context within which they exist (and some of these poems were written with the assistance of the OAC Writers' Reserve program)

to my friends and writing colleagues who form a vital and sustaining community of writers and readers

to my wife, Beth, and our family who remain enablers & inspirers

to Denis De Klerck for the mad sane venture of Mansfield

& especially, to Stuart Ross for his encouraging, perceptive, sensitive, and intelligent editorial insights, which are an essential part of this book

Gary Barwin is a writer, composer, multimedia artist, educator and the author of 16 books of poetry and fiction as well as numerous chapbooks. His work has been widely published and performed both in Canada and internationally. He was Fall 2013 Young Voices eWriter-in-Residence at the Toronto Public Library and was the winner of the 2013 City of Hamilton Arts Award (Writing), the Hamilton Poetry Book of the Year 2011, and co-winner of 2011 Harbourfront Poetry NOW competition, the 2010 bpNichol Chapbook Award, and the KM Hunter Artist Award. He also recently received major grants from the Canada Council and the Ontario Arts Council for his novel-in-progress. He has a PhD in music composition and has taught writing courses in many places, including McMaster University, Mohawk College, and through the Art Forms program for street-involved youth. He lives in Hamilton, Ontario, and online at garybarwin.com.

OTHER BOOKS FROM MANSFIELD PRESS

Poetry
Leanne Averbach, *Fever*
Nelson Ball, *In This Thin Rain*
George Bowering, *Teeth: Poems 2006–2011*
Stephen Brockwell, *Complete Surprising Fragments of Improbable Books*
Stephen Brockwell & Stuart Ross, eds., *Rogue Stimulus: The Stephen Harper Holiday Anthology for a Prorogued Parliament*
Diana Fitzgerald Bryden, *Learning Russian*
Alice Burdick, *Flutter*
Alice Burdick, *Holler*
Jason Camlot, *What The World Said*
Margaret Christakos, *wipe.under.a.love*
Pino Coluccio, *First Comes Love*
Dani Couture, *YAW*
Gary Michael Dault, *The Milk of Birds*
Pier Giorgio Di Cicco, *The Dark Time of Angels*
Pier Giorgio Di Cicco, *Dead Men of the Fifties*
Pier Giorgio Di Cicco, *The Honeymoon Wilderness*
Pier Giorgio Di Cicco, *Living in Paradise*
Pier Giorgio Di Cicco, *Early Works*
Pier Giorgio Di Cicco, *The Visible World*
Salvatore Difalco, *What Happens at Canals*
Christopher Doda, *Aesthetics Lesson*
Christopher Doda, *Among Ruins*
Glenn Downie, *Monkey Soap*
Rishma Dunlop, *The Body of My Garden*
Rishma Dunlop, *Lover Through Departure: New and Selected Poems*
Rishma Dunlop, *Metropolis*
Rishma Dunlop & Priscila Uppal, eds., *Red Silk: An Anthology of South Asian Women Poets*
Ollivier Dyens, *The Profane Earth*
Jaime Forsythe, *Sympathy Loophole*
Carole Glasser Langille, *Late in a Slow Time*
Suzanne Hancock, *Another Name for Bridge*
Jason Heroux, *Emergency Hallelujah*
Jason Heroux, *Memoirs of an Alias*
Jason Heroux, *Natural Capital*
John B. Lee, *In the Terrible Weather of Guns*
Jeanette Lynes, *The Aging Cheerleader's Alphabet*
David W. McFadden, *Be Calm, Honey*
David W. McFadden, *Shouting Your Name Down the Well: Tankas and Haiku*
David W. McFadden, *What's the Score?*
Leigh Nash, *Goodbye, Ukulele*
Lillian Necakov, *The Bone Broker*
Lillian Necakov, *Hooligans*
Peter Norman, *At the Gates of the Theme Park*
Peter Norman, *Water Damage*
Natasha Nuhanovic, *Stray Dog Embassy*
Catherine Owen & Joe Rosenblatt, with Karen Moe, *Dog*
Corrado Paina, *The Alphabet of the Traveler*
Corrado Paina, *The Dowry of Education*
Corrado Paina, *Hoarse Legend*
Corrado Paina, *Souls in Plain Clothes*
Stuart Ross et al., *Our Days in Vaudeville*
Matt Santateresa, *A Beggar's Loom*
Matt Santateresa, *Icarus Redux*
Ann Shin, *The Last Thing Standing*
Jim Smith, *Back Off, Assassin! New and Selected Poems*
Jim Smith, *Happy Birthday, Nicanor Parra*
Robert Earl Stewart, *Campfire Radio Rhapsody*
Robert Earl Stewart, *Something Burned Along the Southern Border*
Carey Toane, *The Crystal Palace*
Priscila Uppal, *Summer Sport: Poems*
Priscila Uppal, *Winter Sport: Poems*
Steve Venright, *Floors of Enduring Beauty*
Brian Wickers, *Stations of the Lost*

Fiction
Marianne Apostolides, *The Lucky Child*
Sarah Dearing, *The Art of Sufficient Conclusions*
Denis De Klerck, ed., *Particle & Wave: A Mansfield Omnibus of Electro-Magnetic Fiction*
Paula Eisenstein, *Flip Turn*
Sara Heinonen, *Dear Leaves, I Miss You All*
Marko Sijan, *Mongrel*
Tom Walmsley, *Dog Eat Rat*

Non-Fiction
George Bowering, *How I Wrote Certain of My Books*
Rosanna Caira & Tony Aspler, *Buon Appetito Toronto*
Denis De Klerck & Corrado Paina, eds., *College Street–Little Italy: Toronto's Renaissance Strip*
Pier Giorgio Di Cicco, *Municipal Mind: Manifestos for the Creative City*
Amy Lavender Harris, *Imagining Toronto*
David W. McFadden, *Mother Died Last Summer*

For more information on these titles, and to order books, please visit
www.mansfieldpress.net